PIERRE
AND
MARIE CURIE

W
FRANKLIN WATTS
LONDON • SYDNEY

Robyn Hardyman

Franklin Watts
First published in Great Britain in 2016 by The Watts Publishing Group

Credits
Produced by Calcium
Series Editors: Sarah Eason and Jennifer Sanderson
Series Designer: Keith Williams
Picture researcher: Rachel Blount

Photo credits: Cover: Library of Congress: George Grantham Bain Collection (right); Wikimedia
Commons: Dujardin (left); Inside: Dreamstime: A40757 27, Amoklv 45, Bananaboy 19, Chaoss 42,
Fotoluminate 26, Frantab01 39, Tine Grebenc 22, Georgios Kollidas 30, Daniel Lesniak 44c, Nexus7 43,
Dana Rothstein 23, Tarczas 1, 16, Warczakoski 44r; Flickr: Rosefirerising 5; Library of Congress: 24, 36,
37, 41, H.W. Cherry 25, Detroit Publishing Co. 7, George Grantham Bain Collection 4, 28, 32, 34; Musée
Curie: Sacha Lenormand 38; Shutterstock: BlueRingMedia 21, Zbynek Burival 20, IgorGolovniov 18,
Marekusz 6, MNI 13, Neftali 33, Rook76 15, Georgy Shafeev 12, Roman Sigaev 3; Wikimedia Commons: 8,
14, 17, Benjamin Couprie 35, Billy Hathorn 31, LOC/Lucien Baylac 10, Mbzt 11, Paul Nadar/Smithsonian
Institution Libraries 17, Nihil Novi 9, Stannered 29.

Dewey number: 540.9'22
ISBN: 978 1 4451 4483 2

Printed in China

FSC
www.fsc.org

MIX
Paper from
responsible sources
FSC® C104740

Franklin Watts
An imprint of
Hachette Children's Group
Part of The Watts Publishing Group
Carmelite House
50 Victoria Embankment
London EC4Y 0DZ

An Hachette UK Company
www.hachette.co.uk

www.franklinwatts.co.uk

Contents

CHAPTER 1

A Remarkable Couple

When asked to name a female scientist, most people say one name – Marie Curie (1867–1934). Marie Curie was born in Poland but lived most of her life in France. It was there that she met another scientist, the Frenchman Pierre Curie (1859–1906). Together they made some of the most important scientific discoveries of the twentieth century.

The life of Marie Curie is a story of determination. Unable to receive the education she longed for in Poland, she worked to raise money so that she could travel to Paris, France. There she battled against prejudice towards women scientists at almost every stage of her career. However, her incredible work soon began to speak for itself.

From a young age, Marie showed the determination and the serious approach to her work that made her such a remarkable scientist.

Pierre Curie was Marie's partner in work as well as in life. They were devoted to each other, and to pursuing their scientific goals.

Generous in sharing

Marie's life and work would have been completely different without her husband and co-researcher, Pierre Curie. He was already a talented scientist when they met and together they ventured into new areas of science. They were determined to work hard and to perfect their scientific method. They were always willing to share their discoveries freely and were more interested in the next piece of research than in making money.

IN THEIR OWN WORDS

The Curies were always looking for funding for their work. When Pierre was offered the highest award available in France, the Legion of Honour, in 1903, he replied:

'I pray to thank the Minister, and to inform him that I do not in the least feel the need of a decoration, but that I do feel the greatest need for a laboratory.'

Marie's Early Life

Marie's early childhood was happy. However, before she became a teenager, tragedy struck and her life changed forever.

Marie was born Maria Sklodowska in Warsaw, Poland, on the 7 November 1867. She was the youngest of five children. Her family lived in a school for girls, where their mother was the headmistress. It was quite unusual for a woman of her social position to have a career. Maria's father was a scientist. When he got a job teaching physics in a boys' school, the family moved to a flat there. Their mother gave up her own job but she worked very hard teaching her children at home. Maria grew up with this example of hard work and the importance of learning.

This is the house in Warsaw where Maria was born. Her family lived in a flat behind the classrooms.

When Maria was growing up, Poland was under foreign rule, and Warsaw (below) was governed by Russia. Maria's family longed for Poland to become independent.

Two terrible blows

During Maria's childhood, Russia controlled part of Poland, including Warsaw. Maria's parents supported Polish independence and, as a result, her father lost his teaching job. This misfortune was then followed by tragedy when Maria's oldest sister caught typhus and died. Fewer than three years later, when Maria was still only 10 years old, her mother died from tuberculosis. Maria was devastated by grief and her sadness stayed with her throughout her life. However, the loss made her determined to make something of her own life.

IN THEIR OWN WORDS

Later in her life, Maria said:

'I was taught that the way of progress was neither swift nor easy.'

A Determined Young Woman

Science was Maria's passion and from a young age she excelled at it. She was determined to get to university, but it was a struggle.

At the age of 15, Maria finished secondary school at the top of her class. Women were not allowed to study at Warsaw University so Maria made a pact with her older sister, Bronisława (1865–1939). Maria would work as a governess to raise money for Bronisława to study medicine in Paris. Once Bronisława qualified as a doctor, she would pay for Maria to study in Paris. Maria spent several years as a governess and finally, in 1891, she boarded the train to Paris.

Maria (far left, with her sisters Bronisława and Helena [1866–1961]) adored her father. He was a scientist and physics teacher but, sadly, could not afford to pay for his daughters' studies in Paris, which caused him great sadness.

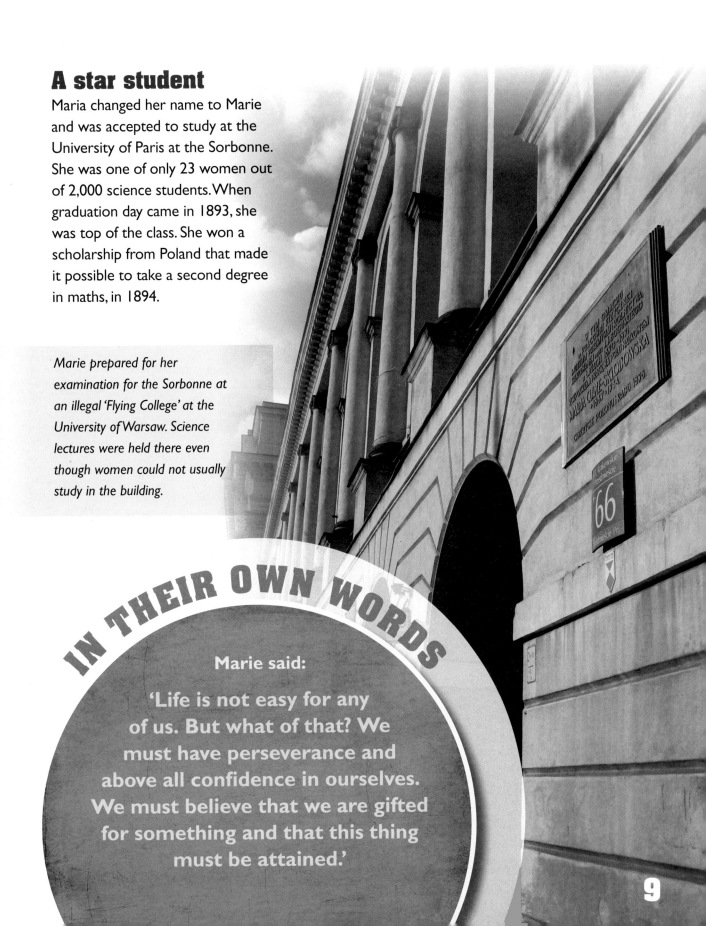

A star student

Maria changed her name to Marie and was accepted to study at the University of Paris at the Sorbonne. She was one of only 23 women out of 2,000 science students. When graduation day came in 1893, she was top of the class. She won a scholarship from Poland that made it possible to take a second degree in maths, in 1894.

Marie prepared for her examination for the Sorbonne at an illegal 'Flying College' at the University of Warsaw. Science lectures were held there even though women could not usually study in the building.

IN THEIR OWN WORDS

Marie said:

'Life is not easy for any of us. But what of that? We must have perseverance and above all confidence in ourselves. We must believe that we are gifted for something and that this thing must be attained.'

Pierre's Parisian Childhood

Pierre Curie was born and grew up in Paris. His early life followed a predictable route for the son of a doctor, but his talent soon marked him for a successful career of his own.

Pierre Curie was born on 15 May 1859. It was clear that he was academically gifted from an early age, and his father decided that he should be educated at home. Although he was brilliant at maths, he had difficulty with accurately writing things down. Today, we would say Pierre was dyslexic.

Paris at the end of the nineteenth century looked rather different from today. The Eiffel Tower had just been built beside the River Seine.

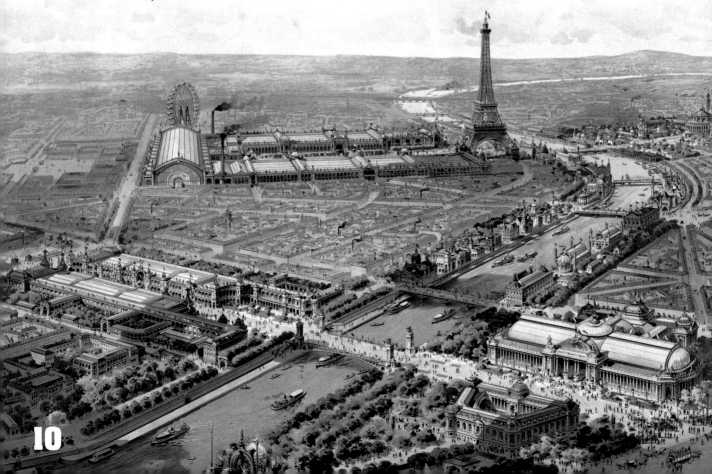

This is the École Supérieure de Chimie Industrielle in Paris. It is where Pierre Curie worked.

Laboratory work

When Pierre was just 16 years old he earned a degree in maths. By the age of 18, he had the equivalent of a higher degree. It was logical for him to carry on his studies but his family did not have enough money for him to do his doctorate. Instead, Pierre began working in a science laboratory as an instructor. He would spend the rest of his career in one science laboratory after another, but as a pioneer rather than an employee.

BEHIND THE SCIENCE

Paris in the late nineteenth century was a centre of science and technology. The prestigious French Academy of Sciences had been open since 1666. It awarded important prizes for research, and this directed scientists' work towards groundbreaking areas. Pierre was elected to the Academy in 1905.

Piezoelectricity

Pierre worked closely with his brother, Jacques (1856–1941). Together they studied quartz crystals and electricity, and made an amazing discovery. The results of their work had a major effect on the development of electronics in the twentieth century.

Pierre and Jacques developed a good understanding of the structure of quartz crystals. In 1880, they found that when these quartz crystals were heavily compressed, a small amount of electric charge was created inside them. They called this piezoelectricity after the Greek word 'piezo', which means to squeeze or press. Piezoelectricity was fascinating to other physicists. When one physicist suggested that the process might be able to be reversed, Pierre and Jacques demonstrated that it could be. The crystals could be made to deform in shape when they were exposed to electricity, without being physically squeezed. To help with their work, Pierre and Jacques invented a machine to measure the electricity, called a Piezoelectric Quartz Electrometer.

This picture shows the surface of a piece of silicon that has had a laser beamed onto it. It was taken using a very powerful microscope that uses piezoelectricity.

We use piezoelectricity every time we light a flame with a lighter like this one. Since the Curies' discovery of piezoelectricity, it has been developed and put to thousands of different uses. Strong demand for it comes from medical instruments and IT devices. In 2013, the global demand for piezoelectric devices was valued at approximately £11.75 billion.

Modern uses

The theory of piezoelectricity has been used in many different types of technology. Modern scanning probe microscopes that can magnify objects thousands of times use it. Microphones, quartz watches and various medical instruments also use it, but the biggest use is in electronics. In our modern digital world, almost all digital electronic circuits rely on piezoelectricity.

BEHIND THE SCIENCE

One day, the piezoelectric effect may be used to harvest wind energy. Scientists have made bendable filaments that produce a charge when blown by the wind.

CHAPTER 2

Working Together

In 1894, Pierre and Marie met by chance in Paris. What developed was not only a great love but also a great meeting of minds. It was a partnership of genius, and their scientific collaboration would have a huge impact on the world.

Marie's professor had given her a project to study the magnetism of steel. The only problem was that she had nowhere to work. A friend of Marie's from Poland suggested she contact a friend of his, who was working on magnetism. His name was Pierre Curie. Both Marie and Pierre had had one previous unhappy experience of love, and had decided to devote themselves to their work instead. However, they began to fall in love with each other. Their personalities were similar – both were quiet, studious and dedicated. In July 1895, they were married.

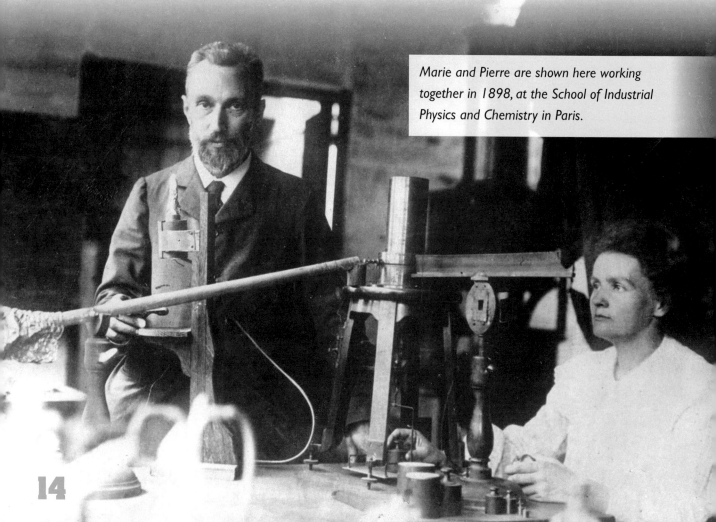

Marie and Pierre are shown here working together in 1898, at the School of Industrial Physics and Chemistry in Paris.

40F POSTES

Professor Curie

Pierre had never completed a doctorate. Marie believed the work he had been doing on magnetism was important and she persuaded him to submit it. He was awarded his degree and finally made a professor of physics at the Sorbonne. Pierre had discovered that a material's magnetic properties change at different temperatures. The temperature at which those properties change is today called the Curie Point, after Pierre.

IN THEIR OWN WORDS

In 1894, Pierre Curie wrote to Marie:

'[In science] we can aspire to accomplish something ... every discovery, however small, is a permanent gain.'

X-rays and Uranium

Marie was looking for a subject for her doctorate. She was fascinated by the work of Wilhelm Röntgen (1845–1923) who, in 1895, had discovered X-rays. Henri Becquerel (1852–1908) had discovered another type of mysterious ray. His work drew her attention even more.

X-rays are beams of light that can pass through flesh and show people's bones. Röntgen had taken the first ever X-ray photograph of his wife's hand. Becquerel's rays were different. He found that the metal uranium, even if kept in the dark, gave off rays that would mist up a photographic plate. He had discovered this by accident but he reported it to the French Academy of Sciences. His findings did not create much of a response at first. Everyone was more interested in Röntgen's X-rays.

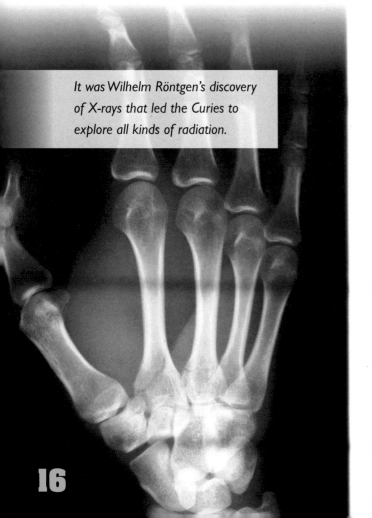

It was Wilhelm Röntgen's discovery of X-rays that led the Curies to explore all kinds of radiation.

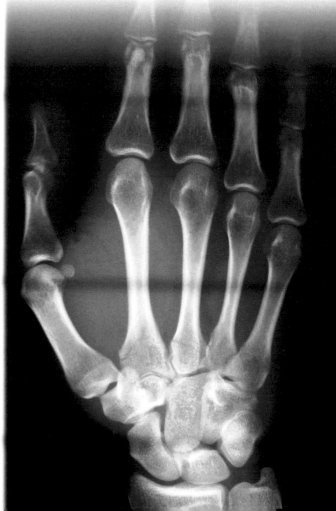

Henri Becquerel was a French scientist. His grandfather and father were physicists, and so was his son. He discovered the rays given off by uranium by accident, while exploring phosphorescence. This is a process by which a material gives off light of one colour after being exposed to light of another colour.

BEHIND THE SCIENCE

During the late nineteenth century, no woman anywhere in the world had ever been awarded a doctorate in science. Marie Curie was determined to be the first.

A busy life

Marie Curie was interested in Becquerel's work. She needed a subject that would not have a long history to research because her life was so busy. She was researching and also working as a teacher. She wanted to teach science to other young women, to encourage them to pursue their careers. Marie even gave back scholarship money she had received from Poland several years before so that another Polish student could benefit from it.

An Equal Partnership

Marie wanted to start investigating Becquerel's mysterious rays. She had found her life's partner and her life's work. Pierre was always there to work tirelessly alongside Marie.

Becquerel thought that the rays given off by uranium were creating an electric current. Marie wanted to study these currents. She was given a small, damp storeroom at Pierre's place of work, the School of Industrial Physics and Chemistry, to use as a laboratory. The electrometer that Pierre had invented for his work on piezoelectricity was perfect for measuring this very low level current.

The Curies' was a perfect partnership: Marie could not have measured the tiny electric currents given off by the materials she was examining without the use of Pierre's electrometer, similar to the illustration shown here.

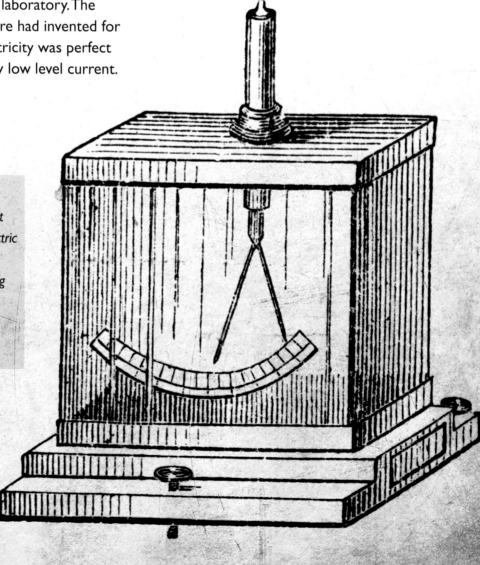

The dangers of radioactivity were not understood for many years. Eventually this symbol was devised as the danger classification sign for radioactive materials.

A revolutionary idea

Marie studied the uranium rays carefully. She invented a new word for the behaviour of uranium – radioactivity. Marie was not sure, but it seemed that the only explanation was that radioactivity came from within the uranium atoms themselves. It would later become clear that radiation actually consisted of particles smaller than an atom – sub-atomic particles (see page 28).

BEHIND THE SCIENCE

In the nineteenth century, it was unusual for women to have a career after they married, but Pierre never expected that Marie would give up her work. In 1897, their first baby, Irène, was born and their lives became even busier. Marie found it difficult to cope with so many demands on her time and energy. When Pierre's mother died, it was decided that his father would live with them. He managed the household and developed a strong bond with his granddaughter.

CHAPTER 3

New Elements

As she continued her studies on uranium, Marie knew she was onto something big. She wanted to know if other substances could give off the radioactivity that she had observed.

Chemists in Paris sent Marie samples of every different known mineral to test. She soon found that any compound containing uranium was radioactive. The element thorium and its compounds were radioactive, too. It was one particular compound of uranium that held the key to Marie's progress. It was called pitchblende. Pitchblende seemed to be even more radioactive than just uranium alone.

Pitchblende is a radioactive black ore. Marie was sent several tonnes of it by the Austrian government, where it was a waste product.

This illustration shows a radioactive element called polonium. It was discovered by the Curies. It has few uses because its radioactivity makes it so dangerous.

A good result

Pierre gave up his work on crystals to join Marie in the quest to understand pitchblende. It was painstaking work to isolate all the different substances in pitchblende and measure the electric current given off by each one. In July 1898, the Curies published their findings. They had found a tiny amount of a new element. They called it 'polonium' after Marie's home country, Poland.

IN THEIR OWN WORDS

Marie described their work isolating polonium:

'We chose, for our work, the ore pitchblende, a uranium ore, which in its pure state is about four times more active than oxide of uranium. Since the composition of this ore was known through very careful chemical analysis, we could expect to find, at a maximum, one per cent of new substance. The result of our experiment proved that there were in reality new radioactive elements in pitchblende, but that their proportion did not reach even a millionth per cent!'

Another Element

The Curies continued with their work in what Marie called their 'miserable old shed'. Before long, Marie had identified another new element.

The reaction among the scientists of Paris to Marie's discovery of polonium was amazement. Here was a woman scientist announcing a new element to be added to the list of those already known, called the Periodic Table. Before the end of that year, Marie had another announcement to make. She had identified a second new element. She called this one 'radium', from the Latin word for 'ray'.

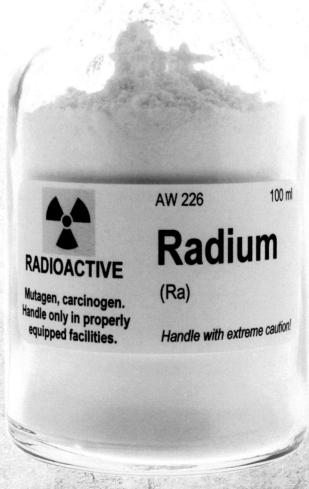

Radium is a pure white metal, but when it is exposed to air it turns black. It glows a faint blue colour which is visible in the dark.

AW 226   100 ml

RADIOACTIVE

Radium

(Ra)

Mutagen, carcinogen. Handle only in properly equipped facilities.

Handle with extreme caution!

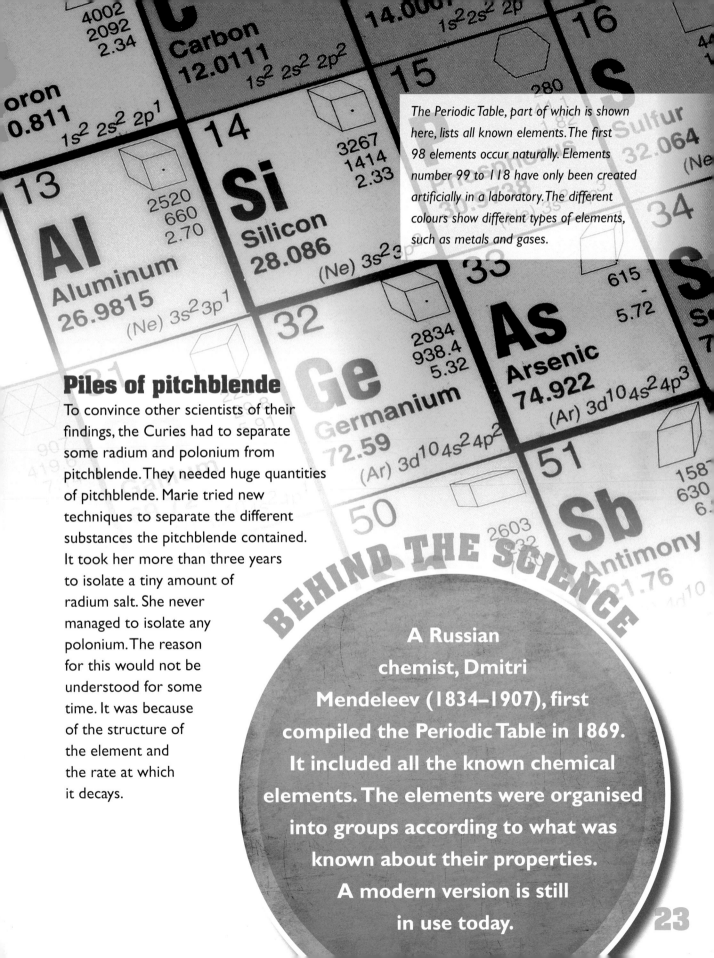

The periodic table background shows several elements:

Carbon
12.0111
$1s^2 2s^2 2p^2$

oron
0.811
$1s^2 2s^2 2p^1$

13
Al
2520
660
2.70
Aluminum
26.9815
$(Ne) 3s^2 3p^1$

14
Si
3267
1414
2.33
Silicon
28.086
$(Ne) 3s^2 3p$

15

16
S
Sulfur
32.064

32
Ge
2834
938.4
5.32
Germanium
72.59
$(Ar) 3d^{10} 4s^2 4p^2$

33
As
615
-
5.72
Arsenic
74.922
$(Ar) 3d^{10} 4s^2 4p^3$

34

50
2603

51
Sb
1587
630
Antimony
121.76

Piles of pitchblende

To convince other scientists of their findings, the Curies had to separate some radium and polonium from pitchblende. They needed huge quantities of pitchblende. Marie tried new techniques to separate the different substances the pitchblende contained. It took her more than three years to isolate a tiny amount of radium salt. She never managed to isolate any polonium. The reason for this would not be understood for some time. It was because of the structure of the element and the rate at which it decays.

BEHIND THE SCIENCE

A Russian chemist, Dmitri Mendeleev (1834–1907), first compiled the Periodic Table in 1869. It included all the known chemical elements. The elements were organised into groups according to what was known about their properties. A modern version is still in use today.

23

Radiant Radium

Marie and Pierre were delighted with their discoveries. Sitting on the shelves of their broken-down shed were jars full of glowing substances. Their secrets were just waiting to be unlocked.

Radium is 2 million times more radioactive than uranium. It glows brightly in the dark and makes nearby materials glow, too. This is because it makes them radioactive by giving off a radioactive gas called radon. Radium gives off heat, too. It gives off enough heat to boil a cup of cold water if it is dropped into it!

Radium was put into the paints used on clock faces so that the marks would glow in the dark. When the women in the factories who used the paints became ill, the problem was eventually traced back to the radium.

In the frenzy to make use of the new radium, all kinds of products containing it were rapidly developed.

This hair product from 1924, containing radium, was used to produce long-lasting curls in the user's hair.

A hidden danger

Radium burns whatever it touches. In the Curies' shed, this included their skin and clothes. Marie and Pierre were in danger – their whole workshop was contaminated with radiation, and unknown to them, it was beginning to make them ill.

The world was soon fascinated by radium. People thought it was a miracle cure for all diseases. It was put into face creams and medicines of all kinds. The Curies made no money from these products and they shared the secret of how to extract radium with everybody.

Our New Radium $5.00 Permanent Wave Beauty

COPYRIGHT 1924 H.W. CHERRY SUSSMAN

International Recognition

The Curies were on the brink of worldwide fame. France may have been a little slow to honour the couple, but the rest of the world was not.

Pierre Curie had always been something of an outsider in the world of Parisian science. He preferred working in his laboratory to spending time with people who could advance his career. In 1902, he applied to become a member of the Academy of Sciences. He was bitterly disappointed when he was rejected. It was only when the Curies threatened to move to Switzerland that Pierre was offered a better job at the Sorbonne.

The Sorbonne, in Paris, was a major centre of scientific research.

Nobel Prize gold medals have an image of their founder, Alfred Nobel (1833–1896), on them. Winning one is still the highest accolade a scientist can receive.

ALFR·
NOBEL

NAT·
MDCCC
XXXIII
OB·
MDCCC
XCVI

Finding fame

Recognition was around the corner for the Curies, however. In June 1903, Marie submitted her research on radioactivity and was granted a doctorate. She was the first woman ever to receive one in France. The examiners said Marie's research contributed more to scientific knowledge than any before it. In November that year, Marie and Pierre, alongside Becquerel, were awarded the Nobel Prize for physics. They were also invited to the Royal Institution in England to talk about their work. They did not like the media attention they received. Their focus was on work and family. In December 1904, the Curies' second daughter, Eve (1904–2007), was born.

BEHIND THE SCIENCE

The Nobel

Prize was set up by a Swedish scientist called Alfred Nobel. He wanted to reward people who made great achievements in science, medicine, literature and working for peace. Nobel Prizes are still awarded every year.

27

CHAPTER 4

Understanding the Atom

Pierre Curie's work on the properties of radium led to discoveries that changed the face of science in the twentieth century.

Pierre and a student had noticed that a piece of radium they were studying gave off heat continuously. Where was this heat coming from and what were the 'rays' of radioactivity? Other scientists read the Curies' work and wanted answers to these questions. A New Zealander called Ernest Rutherford (1871–1937) thought that the answer must lie in the structure of the radium atoms. He proposed that the radiation was not rays but tiny particles. The atoms gave off these rays because they were constantly decaying and changing.

Ernest Rutherford was working at McGill University in Canada when he met the Curies in Paris. His terms for the three types of radiation – alpha, beta and gamma – remain in use today.

Changing elements

Rutherford eventually worked out that the radium gave off three types of radiation: alpha and beta radiation in the form of particles, and gamma radiation in the form of waves (like light waves). Pierre Curie used his knowledge of magnetism to investigate all three types. If atoms could decay, they must be made of particles even smaller than those being rearranged. When the atoms in an element decayed, the element changed into a different one. The energy released in this process would eventually be harnessed as nuclear energy.

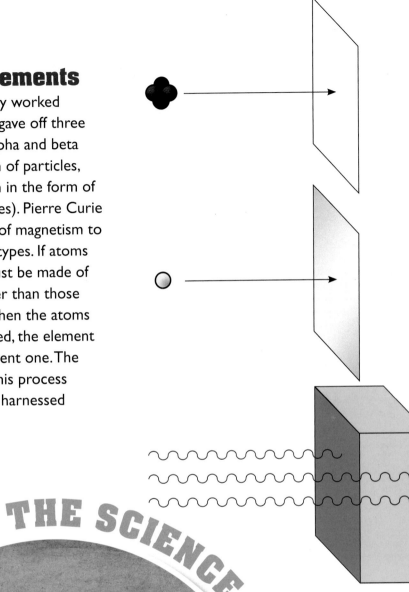

Alpha radiation particles (top) are easily stopped by a sheet of paper. Beta radiation particles (centre) are stopped by an aluminium plate. Gamma radiation rays (bottom) are dampened by lead.

BEHIND THE SCIENCE

As Pierre continued his studies of radium, he became increasingly unwell. He had radium burns on his hands and the effects of radiation were making him ill. This, and the need to respond to pressure from the media, made it difficult for him to work as much as he wanted.

Working Alone

In 1906, tragedy struck the Curies. Life for Marie Curie would never be the same again, but she remained determined to continue the work she and Pierre had begun.

On 19 April 1906, Pierre Curie rushed out into a Parisian street in the rain. Perhaps he was feeling unwell from radiation sickness or perhaps he was deep in thought about the next stage of his work. For whatever reason, he was not looking where he was going. He was hit by a heavy, horse-drawn carriage, and knocked down. He died instantly.

After Pierre's death, Marie felt the grief of any widow, but also the determination of a committed scientist.

IN THEIR OWN WORDS

Marie said of this time:

'Crushed by the blow, I did not feel able to face the future. I could not forget, however, what my husband used to say, that even deprived of him, I ought to continue my work.'

A lasting tribute

Marie was heartbroken. At the age of 38 she had lost her husband, the father of her children and her partner in work. As she had done all through her life, she turned to hard work to find a way through. She had always thought that the French authorities had denied Pierre the recognition he deserved. She was going to fight to create a lasting tribute to him. The Sorbonne offered her Pierre's job as professor of physics, and she accepted. She was determined to set up a state-of-the-art laboratory to carry on his work.

American steel manufacturer and philanthropist Andrew Carnegie (1835–1919) established the Curie Scholarships, which enabled promising scientists to devote themselves full-time to research in Marie's lab.

Difficult Years

The years after Pierre's death were very difficult for Marie. As time went by, however, she found the strength to continue her work and look after her family.

Marie did not think very highly of the French education system. She wanted her girls to receive a good education so in addition to all her other projects, she set up a school to educate them. She joined up with other professional parents.

Each one of them agreed to teach one class each week in their area of expertise. Irène and Eve learned about science, history, literature and maths from some of the most brilliant experts of the time!

As well as her work in the laboratory, Marie (centre) took another job to earn more money, as a teacher. She taught women who were training to become teachers. These are some of her pupils.

The curie

At work, Marie struggled to isolate radium in the form of a metal. In 1910, she finally managed to do it. Also in that year, the International Congress of Radiology and Electricity met in Brussels, Belgium. They needed a name for the brand new unit for measuring radioactivity. The solution was obvious. It was called the curie in Marie and Pierre's honour. In 1911, Marie received another remarkable honour. She won a second Nobel Prize, this time in chemistry, for discovering radium and polonium. She was the first person ever to win two of these distinguished awards.

These are the French winners of the Nobel Prize for Chemistry. The only women are Marie Curie (top row, centre) and her daughter Irène (to the right of her [1897–1956]).

BEHIND THE SCIENCE

Despite all she had achieved, the French Academy still turned down Marie for membership in 1911. It had never had a woman member and was not ready to do so.

CHAPTER 5

A Woman in a Man's World

Marie had taken over Pierre's job as professor of physics but she was still a woman working in a man's world. That particular role was to remain a great struggle for Marie in the next few years.

Marie and Pierre had an old friend, Paul Langevin (1872–1946), who was also a physicist. Now that she was alone, Marie became closer to Langevin and they began a relationship. He was married, however, and when the press became aware of this, there was a terrible scandal. Marie was attacked in the newspapers, and she and her family had to leave their home for safety.

Marie found that a world still dominated by men was not ready to treat her equally when it came to issues of her private life.

The conference in Brussels was known as the Solvay Conference. Marie was the only woman present. Instead of posing for the camera, she continues talking to her neighbour, the physicist Henri Poincaré (1854–1912).

An eminent conference

As before, Marie found comfort in hard work. In 1911, a major world conference for physics was held in Brussels, Belgium. Marie was there, together with other eminent figures such as Ernest Rutherford and Albert Einstein (1879–1955). She was the only woman present. At the same time, the relationship with Langevin came to an end and Marie fled to England. She was ill and depressed. She was looked after by an English friend called Hertha Ayrton (1854–1923), a physicist and campaigner for women's rights. When Marie returned to Paris in 1912, she set her mind to her great challenge: to establish the Radium Institute, which would be a fitting tribute to Pierre, and a workplace for herself for the rest of her life.

IN THEIR OWN WORDS

Of the new Radium Institute, Marie wrote to the Dean of the Sorbonne:

'I have been led to think that there is a public service to be organised, which I cannot ignore, and that it could not have been properly established without myself and my laboratory's participation.'

War Work

In August 1914, just as the Radium Institute was completed on the newly-named Rue Pierre Curie in Paris, the world was plunged into World War I. The work of the Institute would have to wait.

As German troops invaded north-east France, the French government left Paris. Marie took her precious supply of radium, the only radium in France, south to Bordeaux to keep it safe. On the train she held the precious radium on her lap in a lead box. Then, she returned to Paris to see what she could do to help with the war effort.

Marie and her team visited countless field hospitals such as this one in the ruins of a church in France.

Lifesaving X-rays

Marie knew that X-rays could help to save injured soldiers' lives by showing doctors their injuries more clearly. She set up 20 mobile radiology units in trucks and quickly learned how to drive. She trained her daughter, Irène, to be her assistant. She persuaded generals to let her take the trucks to the front lines of the battle, where they were needed most. Despite the dangers from radiation exposure, mother and daughter spent years doing this important work. Marie trained a team of women radiologists to help them. The X-ray trucks became known by the soldiers as 'Petites Curies', meaning 'Little Curies'. They saved countless lives.

The Red Cross tended to wounded soldiers, but with limited diagnostic tools, many lives could not be saved.

BEHIND THE SCIENCE

When the government asked people to hand in their gold and silver for the war effort, Marie offered all her medals, including the two Nobel medals. Her offer was refused.

Radium and Cancer

When the war ended, Marie could finally take up her post as Director of the Radium Institute. Pierre's pioneering work on the properties of radium had shown that it could affect living tissue. This would be put to good use in finding treatments for cancer and other diseases.

As well as conducting pure research into the physics of radioactivity, Marie wanted the medical uses of her work to be developed. This cost money.

In 1920, she set up The Curie Foundation to raise funds for obtaining radium. Radium was needed to create the radiation used in treating cancer patients.

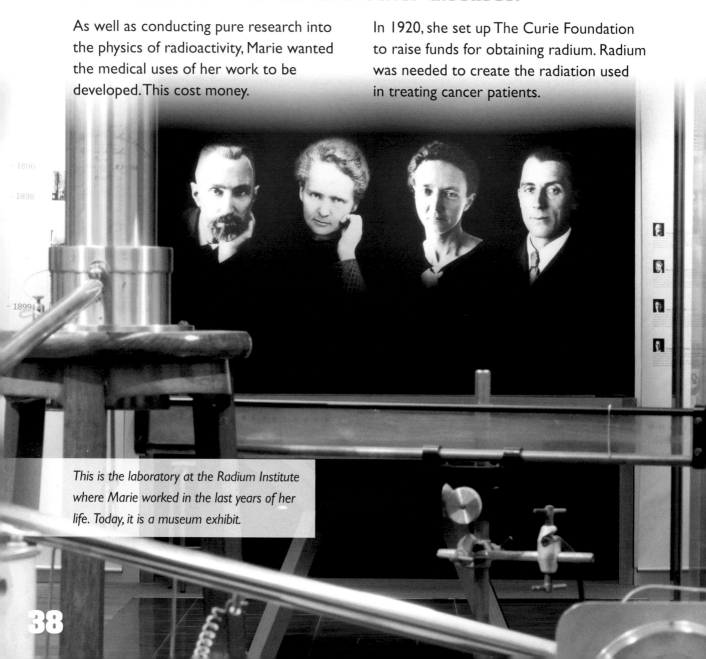

This is the laboratory at the Radium Institute where Marie worked in the last years of her life. Today, it is a museum exhibit.

An effective treatment

Although radiation damages the body and can cause cancers, Marie thought it could also be used to cure cancers. Used in measured doses and delivered directly to the site of the cancer, it kills the cancer cells. In the earliest treatments, small glass tubes were filled with radon gas collected from radium and placed on the patient. Later, needles containing radium were inserted into the tumours. Marie's treatment centre became the model for cancer treatment centres around the world in the early twentieth century.

Radiotherapy forms the basis of many people's treatment for cancer. Side effects can include skin damage and hair loss.

IN THEIR OWN WORDS

Marie said:

'It may be easily understood how deeply I appreciated the privilege of realising that our discovery had become a benefit to mankind . . . by its power of efficient action against human suffering and terrible disease. This was indeed a splendid reward for our years of hard toil.'

CHAPTER 6

Worldwide Acclaim

Universities and institutions around the world heaped honours on Marie Curie. Marie saw this as an opportunity to raise money for The Curie Foundation and its important work.

Marie had received financial help from industry to supply her laboratories. Now, she sought help from governments and wealthy individuals. In 1920, she met an American journalist called Marie 'Missy' Meloney (1878–1943). Marie told her that research and treatment centres in the United States owned 50 times as much radium as the single gram she had in her own laboratory. Meloney started a campaign to help Marie. She persuaded Marie to write her autobiography for an American publisher.

Marie Meloney, Irène, Marie and Eve shortly after their arrival in the United States in 1921.

The high point of Marie's 1921 tour of the United States was the White House presentation by President Warren G. Harding (centre [1865–1923]). She wore the same black dress she had worn to both Nobel Prize ceremonies.

Visiting the United States

In 1921, Marie, Irène and Eve travelled to the United States. The president himself, Warren G. Harding, presented Marie with a gift of radium. Marie hated all the publicity and handshaking. She often asked her daughters to attend events for her. The trip was a huge success, however. Marie returned home with radium, equipment and money for her work.

A second trip to the United States followed in 1929. This time, Marie gathered funds for the Radium Institute she had founded in her beloved home city, Warsaw. Her sister, Bronisława, was its director.

BEHIND THE SCIENCE

When the French government heard that the American president was giving Marie a gift of radium, they decided to offer her the country's highest award, the Legion of Honour. Marie refused it, just as Pierre had done in 1903.

A Peaceful End

The years of working with radiation were beginning to have an effect on Marie's health. The work of her beloved Radium Institute, however, was going strong.

Marie continued working on her own work, and directing the work of others. She was a generous teacher to her researchers, who included women. Other scientists at the Radium Institute were publishing their groundbreaking work on radioactivity, too. The institute was a world-class facility.

Declining health

Gradually, however, Marie's health declined. She was suffering from a blood disorder, and was nursed by Eve. In 1934, her doctors sent her to the Alps for a rest. She died there on 4 July 1934, aged 66. She was buried beside her beloved husband near Paris.

Marie died in a sanatorium in the French Alps in July 1934.

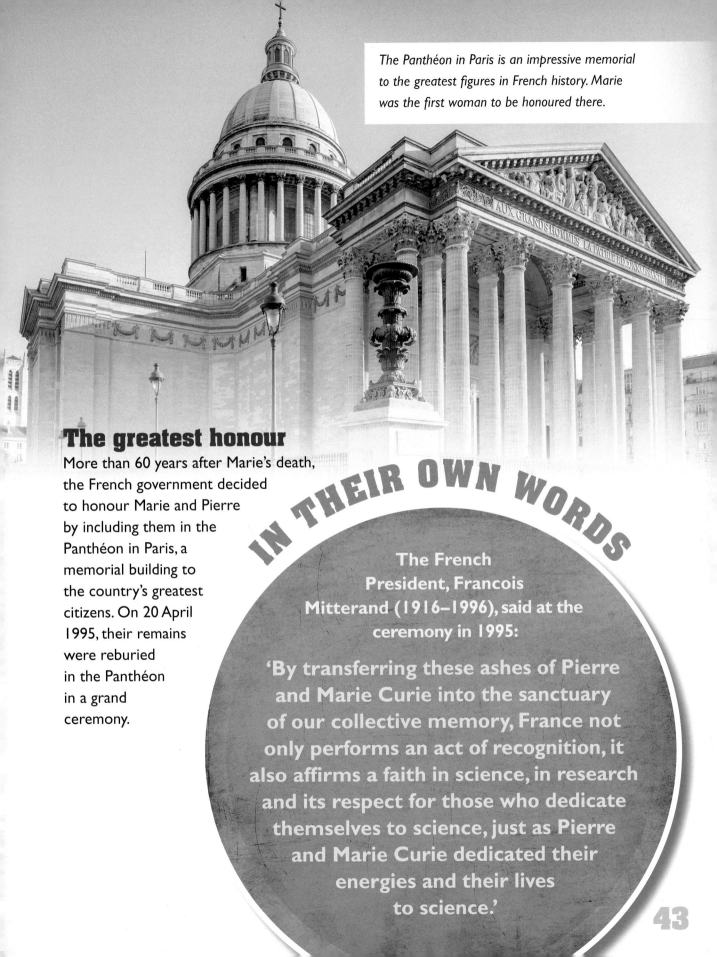

The Panthéon in Paris is an impressive memorial to the greatest figures in French history. Marie was the first woman to be honoured there.

The greatest honour

More than 60 years after Marie's death, the French government decided to honour Marie and Pierre by including them in the Panthéon in Paris, a memorial building to the country's greatest citizens. On 20 April 1995, their remains were reburied in the Panthéon in a grand ceremony.

IN THEIR OWN WORDS

The French President, Francois Mitterand (1916–1996), said at the ceremony in 1995:

'By transferring these ashes of Pierre and Marie Curie into the sanctuary of our collective memory, France not only performs an act of recognition, it also affirms a faith in science, in research and its respect for those who dedicate themselves to science, just as Pierre and Marie Curie dedicated their energies and their lives to science.'

43

A Lasting Legacy

The story of Marie and Pierre Curie is one of patient work, triumph over tragedy and enormous achievement. When they could no longer work together, Marie dedicated her life to continuing the important task of advancing our understanding of science.

Marie lived in a world where women were not expected to have careers, let alone highly successful ones. She took no notice of this and achieved international recognition for her work while also bringing up her daughters. This has inspired many women to follow her example and pursue their own careers. Marie's own family were the first to do this. Irène and her husband shared a Nobel Prize for Chemistry. Their daughter, Marie's granddaughter, was also a scientist.

Poland is proud of its famous sister. This sculpture of Marie Curie stands in Jordan Park, Krakow, Poland. Her birthplace in Warsaw is now a museum dedicated to her life and work.

MARIA
SKŁODOWSKA
CURIE
1867–1934

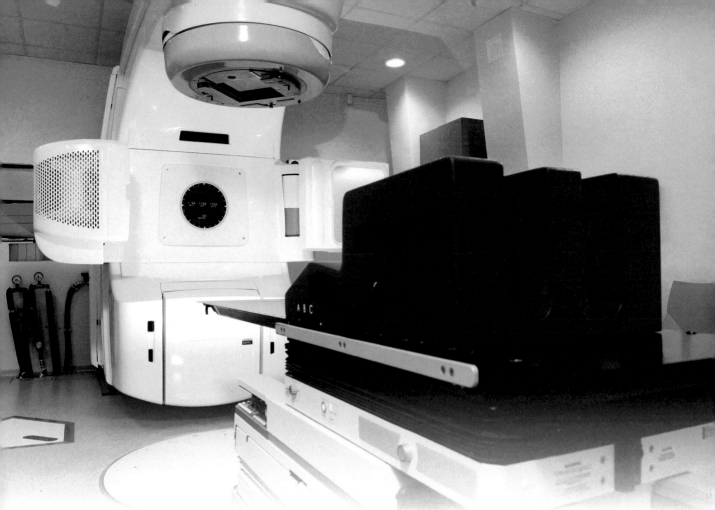

The technology of radiotherapy has come a long way since Marie first discovered radiation, but it remains a powerful, life-saving legacy of her work.

The science continues

The Curies' work furthered research into the structure of the atom, a key building block in the development of physics. The radiation discovered by Marie is used in treating disease and in generating electricity. Today, the Curie Institute remains one of the leading medical and research centres in the world, where many scientists continue the work that was begun by the two remarkable scientists that were Marie and Pierre Curie. That is truly a lasting legacy.

IN THEIR OWN WORDS

Marie Curie said:

'Nothing in life is to be feared, it is only to be understood. Now is the time to understand more, so that we may fear less.'

Glossary

alpha radiation a type of radiation that takes the form of particles

atom the smallest part of an element, which is made up of different types of particles

beta radiation a type of radiation that takes the form of particles

cancer a disease caused by cells multiplying uncontrollably

compound a combination of two or more different elements

compressed squeezed or pressed

current a flow of electricity

doctorate a post-graduate degree completed after a master's degree

element the simplest form of a substance that can not be broken down further, such as carbon, iron or oxygen

gamma radiation a type of radiation that takes the form of rays

governess a woman who teaches children in their own home

laboratory a workshop where scientific experiments are carried out

Nobel Prize a very prestigious international prize awarded every year for an outstanding achievement in an area of science or culture

ore a mineral from which metals can be extracted

particle a very tiny part of something

Periodic Table a diagram showing all the known elements, which are grouped according to their properties

pitchblende a type of rock that contains uranium, polonium and radium

polonium a radioactive metallic element discovered by the Curies in 1898

quartz a mineral found in the ground, often in a crystal form

radioactivity the radiation given out by the decay in the atoms of some elements

radiotherapy using radiation to treat diseases such as cancer

radium a rare, brilliant white radioactive element discovered by Marie Curie

radon the gas given off by radium

sanatorium a place where people are treated for chronic illnesses

tuberculosis an infectious disease that affects the lungs

tumour a growth in the body caused when cells multiply uncontrollably

typhus an infectious disease

uranium a radioactive element; the main element used in nuclear reactors

X-rays energy waves similar to light waves but much shorter

For More Information

Books

Marie Curie (DK Biography), Vicki Cobb, DK Children

Marie Curie (Scientists Who Made History), Liz Gogerly, Wayland

Marie Curie, Philip Steele, QED Publishing

Websites

For an explanation on the three types of radiation, visit:
www.bbc.co.uk/schools/gcsebitesize/science/ocr_gateway_pre_2011/living_future/4_nuclear_radiation1.shtml

Visit this BBC webpage for a short history of Marie Curie:
www.bbc.co.uk/history/historic_figures/curie_marie.shtml

Read about the life and work of Marie Curie at the website for the charity set up in her name for people affected by terminal illness:
www.mariecurie.org.uk/who/our-history/marie-curie-the-scientist

There is a lot of information about the Nobel Prize for physics and the scientists who have won it at:
www.nobelprize.org/nobel_prizes/physics

Note to parents and teachers
Every effort has been made by the Publisher to ensure that these websites contain no inappropriate or offensive material. However, because of the nature of the Internet, it is impossible to guarantee that the contents of these sites will not be altered. We strongly advise that Internet access is supervised by a responsible adult.

Index